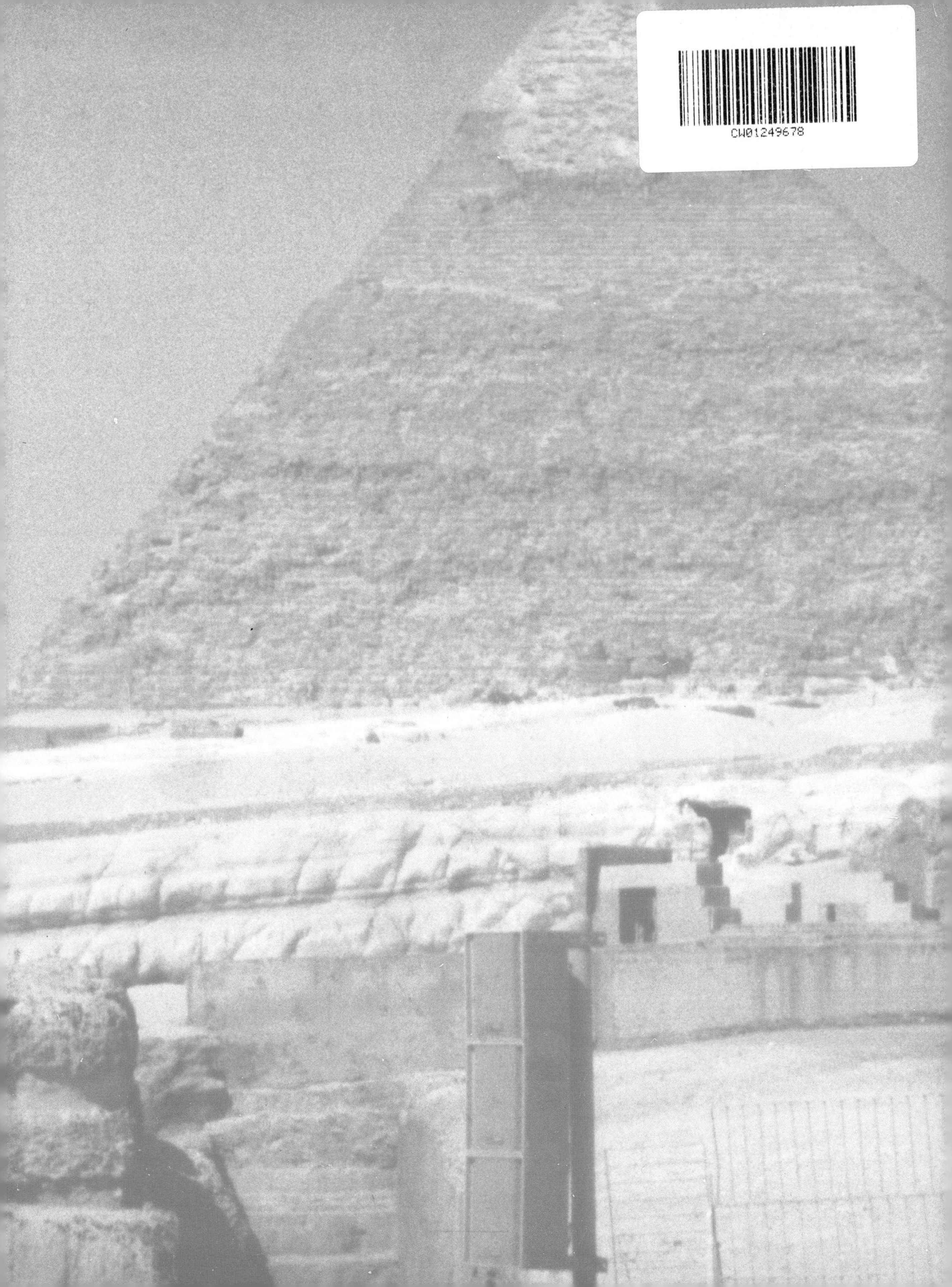

HEADstart

PHARAOHS & MUMMIES

First published in Great Britain by
CAXTON EDITIONS
an imprint of
The Caxton Book Company,
16 Connaught Street,
Marble Arch, London, W2 2AF.

Copyright © 1998 CAXTON EDITIONS

All rights reserved. No part of this publication may be reproduced, stored in a retrieval system, or transmitted, in any form, or by any means, without the prior written permission of the copyright holder.

ISBN 1 84067 022 3

A copy of the CIP data for this book is available from the British Library upon request.

With grateful thanks to Helen Courtney

Created and produced for Caxton Editions by
FLAME TREE PUBLISHING,
a part of The Foundry Creative Media Company Ltd,
Crabtree Hall, Crabtree Lane,
Fulham, London, SW6 6TY.

Printed in Singapore by Star Standard Industries Pte. Ltd.

HEADstart

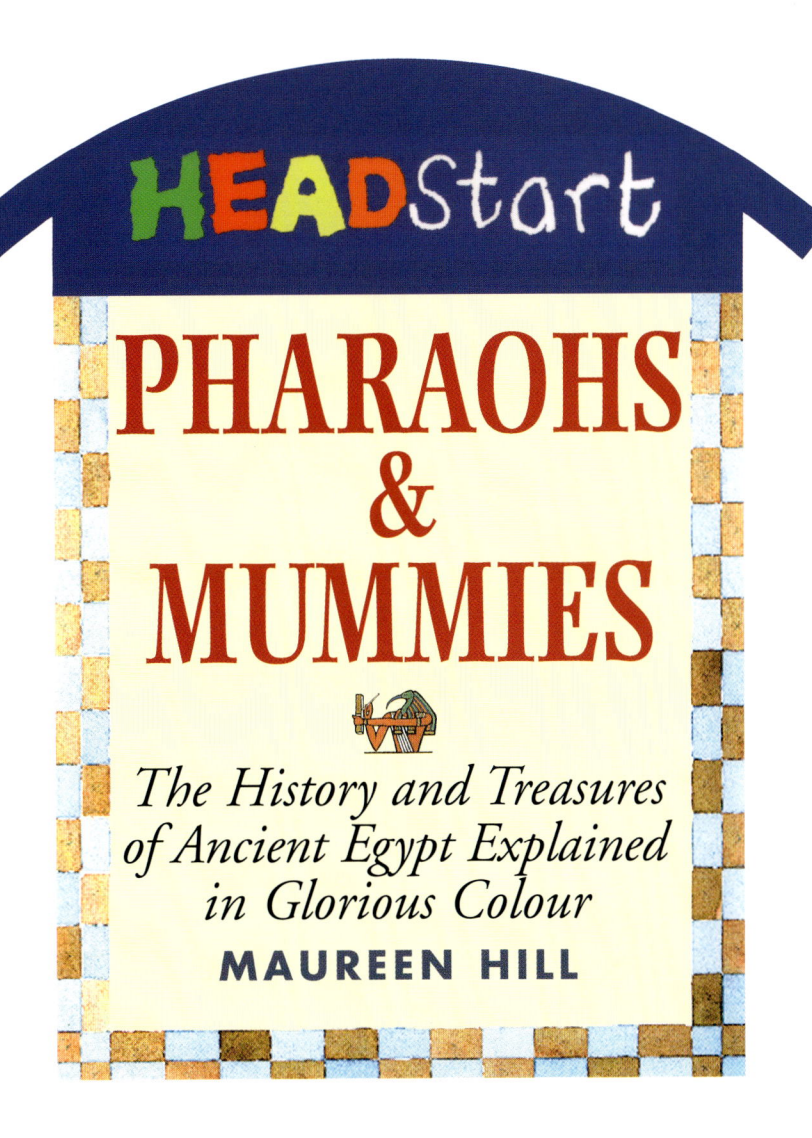

PHARAOHS & MUMMIES

The History and Treasures of Ancient Egypt Explained in Glorious Colour

MAUREEN HILL

Caxton Editions

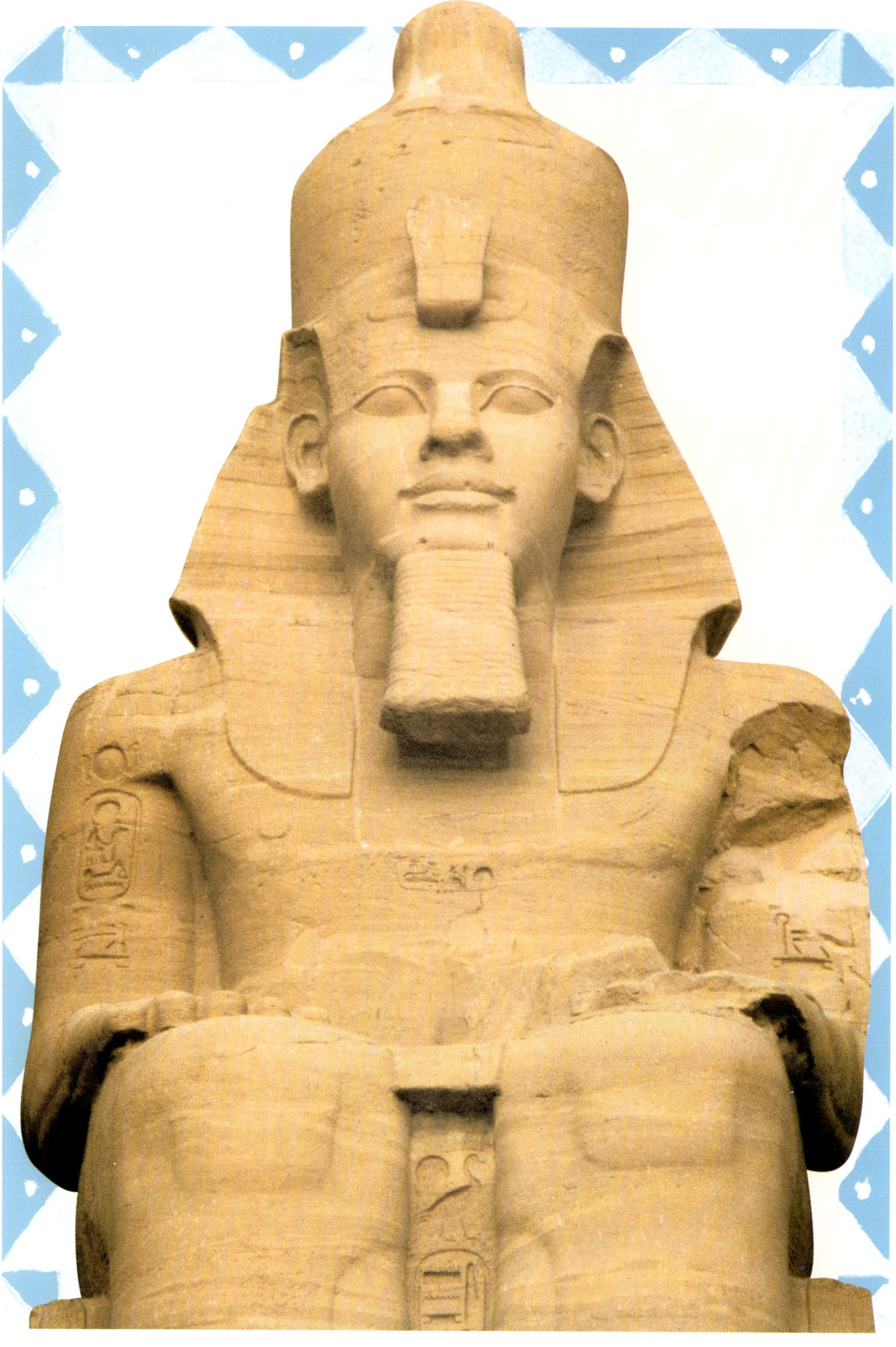

Contents

Introduction	10
Dynasties	12
The Gods	14
The Story of Osiris	16
The Pharaoh	18
Egyptian Society	20
Palace Life	22
Peasant Life	24
Burial Beliefs	26
Mummification	28
Pyramids	30
Burial Goods	32
Grave Robbers	34
The Valley of the Kings	36
Tutenkhamun	38
The Rosetta Stone	40
Cleopatra	42
Further Information and Picture Credits	44

Introduction

Pharaoh means 'great house' and was originally the name given to the palace where the ancient kings of Egypt lived. Eventually it came to be the name given to the king himself.

The first king to rule over all of Egypt was called Menes. He ruled over 5,000 years ago, from the year 3100 BC. The last pharaoh to rule over all of Egypt did so before the birth of Jesus Christ. It is such a long time ago that it is difficult to have exact information about who all the pharaohs were and what life was like at that time.

INTRODUCTION

The Ancient Egyptians preserved the bodies of the pharaohs by a process called 'embalming', then wrapped them up in bandages and put them in special tombs. These remains are called 'mummies'. We have learnt a good deal about the pharaohs and the lives of the Ancient Egyptians from mummies and the tombs they were placed in.

The Ancient Egyptians also left many works of art – paintings and sculptures – that tell us something of their life. They also had a form of writing called 'hieroglyphics', which we are now able to read and understand, and this gives us more information.

'Egyptologists' are people who study ancient Egypt, and over the last hundred years they have made many exciting and interesting discoveries.

Dynasties

The era of Egyptian history during which the pharaohs reigned is called the 'Dynastic Period'. It is divided into five main periods during which the dynasties, or different families, of pharaohs ruled.

The first period was the 'Archaic Period' and lasted from 3100 BC until 2868 BC. It began with the rule of Menes. During this time the Ancient Egyptians developed writing and working with metal.

Following on from the Archaic Period is the 'Old Kingdom' (2868–2181 BC). This is the time during which the Sphinx and the Pyramids were built. Egypt increased its trade with other areas of the world, but war and a collapse of power ended the Old Kingdom.

DYNASTIES

After this there were over a hundred difficult years during which Egypt was not united until, in 2050 BC, the 'Middle Kingdom' was established. Mentuhopte was the pharaoh who reunited Egypt again. It was during this period that the horse-drawn chariot was introduced.

The 'New Kingdom' (1567–1085 BC) followed and this was the period during which Egypt was at its richest and most splendid. The works of art are sophisticated and many are made from precious materials.

The 'Late Period' (1085–332 BC) that followed the New Kingdom was a time of problems for Egypt. It was a time during which several countries conquered Egypt, ending with the conquest of Alexander the Great of Greece.

The Gods

The Ancient Egyptians had many gods. Each area had its own gods but there were several gods who were important throughout the whole kingdom of Egypt. The people built great temples in their honour.

Ra was the creator god. Associated with the sun, he was sometimes called Ra-Atum, Amon-Ra or Ra-Horakhty. Sometimes Ra is portrayed as a falcon, or a man with a falcon's head. Sometimes he is represented as the sun and other times as a scarab beetle. Ra was the father of the twin gods Shu and Tefenet. Shu was god of the air and Tefenet goddess of moisture. Together they created Geb, the god of the earth, and Nut, the goddess of the sky. Geb and Nut were the parents of Osiris, Isis, Seth and Nephthys. Together these nine gods were known as the 'Ennead'.

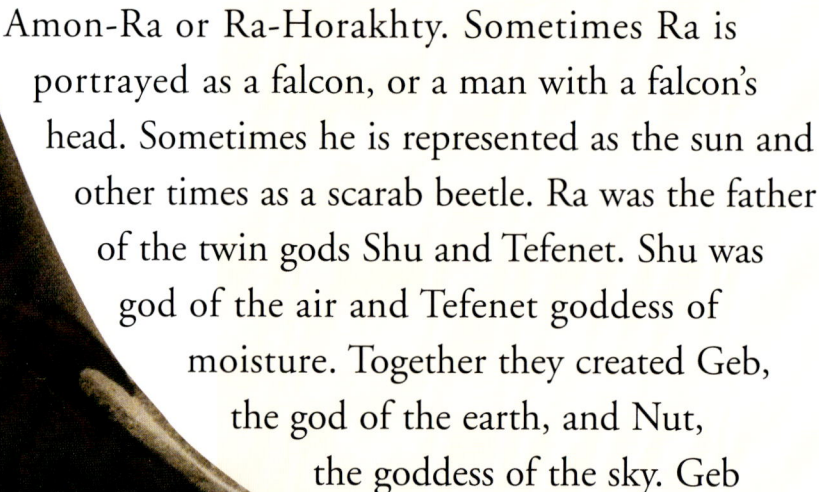

THE GODS

As the creator god, Ra was the father of many other gods. Hathor was another of Ra's daughters. She was goddess of several things – including being the protector of children and the goddess of love. Sometimes she is represented as a cow, or a woman with a cow's head.

Anubis was another of the gods created by Ra. He had the head of a jackal and was guardian of the Underworld.

Pharaoh Amenhotep IV tried to stop the people of Egypt from worshipping all these gods. He believed in a single, all-powerful god called Aten. He even changed his name to Akhenaten which means 'glory to Aten'. The people did not like losing their old gods and when Akhenaten died the new pharaoh, Tutenkhamun, restored the old religion.

The Story of Osiris

One of the most important stories in Ancient Egyptian mythology is the story of Ra's grandchildren, Osiris, Isis and Seth.

Osiris ruled Egypt with Isis, who was his wife and his sister. He was a good and wise ruler, but his jealous brother Seth plotted to kill him and take the throne.

Seth pretended to be friends with Osiris, and invited him to a feast at which he showed Osiris a beautiful chest and said it would belong to whoever could fit inside it. Osiris trusted his brother and got inside the chest. Seth then locked it, sealed it and threw it in to the River Nile.

When Isis heard what had happened, she searched all along the banks of the Nile until she found the chest. Osiris was dead, but Isis took the chest – now her husband's coffin – back to Egypt. Seth was angry that Isis had found it so in the dead of night he took Osiris's body, cut it into fourteen pieces and scattered the parts throughout Egypt.

THE STORY OF OSIRIS

Isis and her sister Nephthys searched for many years to find all the parts of the body. With the help of the god Anubis they put the body back together. Isis and Osiris had one more night together before Osiris went to become king of the Underworld. During that night Isis conceived a baby. She named her son Horus and brought him up secretly until he was old enough to take revenge for Osiris's death.

Horus fought a fierce battle with Seth and the gods decided that Horus should be king. Horus regained the throne of his father Osiris.

The Pharaoh

Pharaohs were believed to be living gods. Every pharaoh was the human form, or 'incarnation', of Horus. When he died he joined Osiris, king of the Underworld.

The pharaoh had to perform daily rituals and services to the gods, which were important to the well-being of all the people of Egypt. The same religious services were performed by priests who acted as the king's deputies in temples throughout the land.

The dress of the pharaoh was important. He would wear a kilt or tunic of 'royal linen', made from the finest threads, often decorated with gold. On his head would be a head-dress of some sort, sometimes a crown. The double crown of Egypt was made up of the white crown of Upper Egypt and the red crown of Lower Egypt. The crown of Lower Egypt had a cobra – a type of snake – on the front. Sometimes a vulture – a symbol of power in Upper Egypt – would appear alongside the cobra.

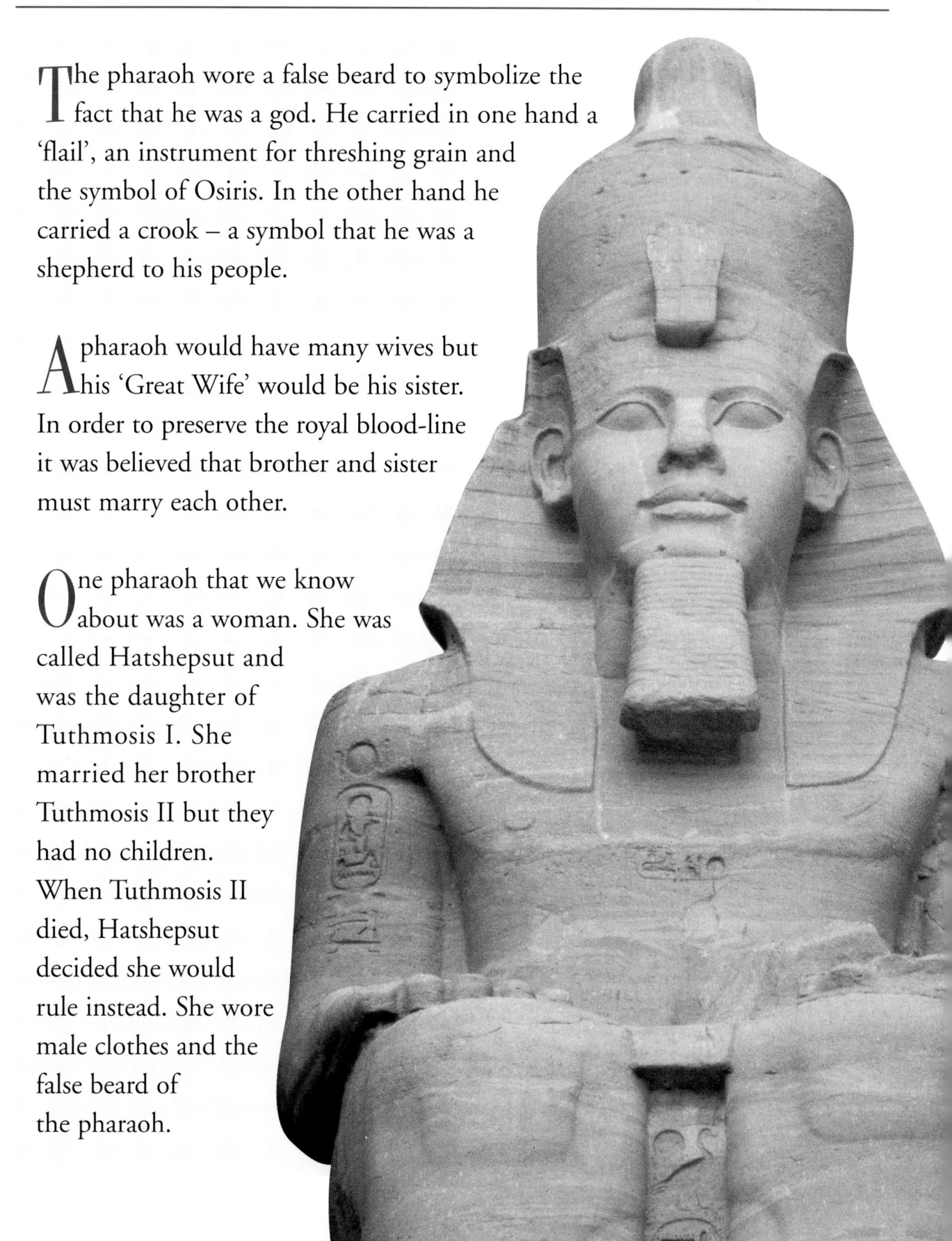

THE PHARAOH

The pharaoh wore a false beard to symbolize the fact that he was a god. He carried in one hand a 'flail', an instrument for threshing grain and the symbol of Osiris. In the other hand he carried a crook – a symbol that he was a shepherd to his people.

A pharaoh would have many wives but his 'Great Wife' would be his sister. In order to preserve the royal blood-line it was believed that brother and sister must marry each other.

One pharaoh that we know about was a woman. She was called Hatshepsut and was the daughter of Tuthmosis I. She married her brother Tuthmosis II but they had no children. When Tuthmosis II died, Hatshepsut decided she would rule instead. She wore male clothes and the false beard of the pharaoh.

Egyptian Society

Ancient Egyptian society was organised rather like a pyramid. At the top of the pyramid was the pharaoh. He was in charge of religion, the army, the law and the government. He was the most important and powerful person in the land.

The pharaoh depended upon a number of people to help him run the country. Just below him in the pyramid were a number of people with power. They were priests, priestesses, nobles and senior government officials. Many of them were relations of the pharaoh. Below this layer were a large number of people responsible for the day-to-day running of the country. These people kept records, collected taxes and dealt with minor crimes.

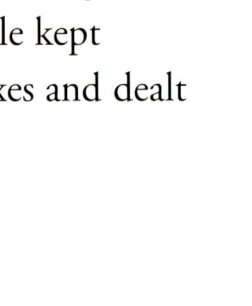

EGYPTIAN SOCIETY

There were two classes below this in the pyramid. First, there were the skilled craftsmen such as metal workers, jewellers, stonemasons, carpenters, artists and makers of pots. Below them were the servants, labourers, who provided the human power to get much of the hard work done, and peasant farmers who produced the food that kept the country going.

The work of the peasant farmers and the fertility of the Nile Valley were the reason that Egypt was such a rich and powerful nation. The River Nile flooded its banks every year with waters from the melting snows in the mountains of Central Africa. These floods left behind rich soil that produced plentiful harvests that fed all the people.

Palace Life

Although the people depended on the protection of the pharaoh, he was kept separate from the people. He lived in a large palace, often close to the temple in which he would carry out his daily religious rituals.

The palace was also important as a seat of government. The pharaoh and his chief government officials would make decisions about the running of the country here.

However, the palace was also where the king lived with his family. Many wives meant the pharaoh often had many children. Rameses II had over 100 children!

The Ancient Egyptians loved good food and celebrations, and the palace saw much of both. Feasts were often held to celebrate harvests or to thank the gods and goddesses. In the palace, served by servants or slaves, the guests would eat from plates and dishes made of silver or gold and drink from cups of the same materials. They would eat with their fingers dishes of roast or stewed meats such as goose or duck and beef, mutton or goat. Fruit such as melon, dates, figs and pomegranates were also eaten, and perhaps also cakes sweetened with honey.

The guests at a feast in the palace would probably have drunk wine. Most Ancient Egyptians made wine out of plums and pomegranates, but it is likely that the pharaoh also served wine made from grapes. In the tomb of Tutenkhamun a jar was found containing the remains of what is believed to be either grape juice or wine.

Peasant Life

The whole land of Egypt belonged to the pharaoh, and peasants had to work on the land. However, they could buy or rent land for their own use. Even slaves or foreigners captured in war could rent land. This meant that in comparison to peasants in many other countries, those in Ancient Egypt lived quite well. The work of farming was hard because, although they may have had some animals to help, most of the work would have been done by the farmer, his wife and children.

The rich land of the Nile flood plain produced plenty of food, and although they had to pay as much of half of the food produced in taxes to the king, there was usually enough for both the tax and the peasant farmer.

PEASANT LIFE

The farmer's house would probably have been made from mud, wood and reeds with the poorest families having only one room in which they ate, slept and lived.

The diet of peasants was much simpler than that of rich people. Bread was the basic food, with beans, lentils and vegetables such as turnips and onions. Radishes, cucumber and lettuces were grown for salads. Hummus, the chickpea dish that we eat today, was also eaten by the Ancient Egyptians.

Beer was the main drink for poorer people. The beer was made by adding bread to water that was then mashed down and left to ferment. It was later strained into jars.

Burial Beliefs

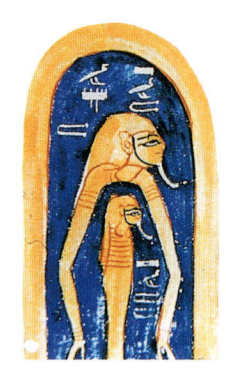

As a farming people the Ancient Egyptians saw that there was a cycle to the growth of crops. They saw the harvest each year, followed by the period when the land was dead, only for the crops to grow again the next year. They believed that human life followed the same cycle.

When a person died they believed that they would come to life again in the afterlife or 'Underworld'. Instead of being with Horus, the living god in Egypt, they would be with Osisris, the king of the Underworld. Here, life would be an idealised version of the life they had lived on earth.

The spirit of the dead person was called the 'ka' and the ka would need the body of its original owner in the Underworld. It was also believed that the name of the dead person must continue to exist after their death, and that they should be given regular supplies of food and drink.

The body was mummified to preserve it. In the tomb where the mummified body was placed, writing the dead person's name on the walls ensured that their name lived on. Paintings or models of farming and food preparation or of the actual food itself were believed to supply the dead person's needs through magic.

BURIAL BELIEFS

Before the mummy was placed in the tomb a ceremony called 'The Opening of the Mouth' was conducted. The mouth of the mummy was touched by a tool to allow the ka to re-enter the body through the mouth and allow the person to be reborn into the afterlife.

The Ancient Egyptians believed that before a person could enter the Underworld they must have their heart weighed against a feather to see how pure it was. The god Anubis judged this. If it was heavier than the feather a monster swallowed it and it became an evil spirit.

Mummification

As farmland was precious, the early Ancient Egyptians buried their dead in the desert. They discovered that the dry sand sucked the moisture from the body and helped preserve it. From this early discovery a complex process of mummification was developed.

Sand did not leave the body looking very lifelike, so a substance called 'natron', a mixture of salt, sodium bicarbonate and sodium carbonate was used to dry the body out.

Priests prepared the body for burial. First the brain was removed from the body by pulling it through the nostrils with a special instrument. It was thought worthless and thrown away. The heart, believed to be the most precious part of the body, was removed with the other internal organs through a long cut in the stomach. All these organs were preserved.

The heart was later returned to the body. The lungs, liver, stomach and intestines were stored in four jars called 'canopic jars'.

The body and the organs were covered with natron and left for 40 days to dry out. The heart was then replaced within the body, which was stuffed with linen to help give it shape.

Next the body was wrapped in strips of linen. Between the layers of the wrapping, special protective charms or 'amulets' were placed to help keep the body safe. Prayers were said over the body.

The mummy was then placed in a specially-fitted wooden coffin. Many of these coffins were beautifully painted and decorated, sometimes with a portrait of the dead person.

Pyramids

The pyramids are the tombs of pharaohs from the Old and the Middle Kingdoms.

The early pyramids were stepped, not smooth-sided. Later on, the steps were filled in with stone and the smooth-sided pyramid we associate with Egypt came about.

The building of pyramids was a huge job. It is estimated that the Great Pyramid at Giza that was built for King Cheops (also called Khufu) took 23 years to complete, and had about 4,000 people working on it.

The pyramids were mostly built from limestone. The rather dull and rough surface we see nowadays was originally finished with fine limestone and polished. Sometimes they were finished with granite. The burial chambers deep within the pyramid were often built of granite, as was the stone coffin, called a 'sarcophagus', in which the wooden coffin was placed.

Granite is a very hard stone and it is difficult to cut. The Ancient Egyptians did this by hammering holes in it with a special hammer, wedging pieces of wood in the holes and then soaking the wood. As the wooden pegs expanded they split the granite. The limestone could be cut and shaped with the copper tools they used.

All pyramids are positioned to face the main points of the compass. The Ancient Egyptians did not have a compass and so had to do use the positions of the stars to locate the pyramids correctly.

The huge blocks of stone were moved over land on sledges dragged over rollers. To place the blocks in position earth ramps were built up the sides of the pyramids.

Burial Goods

The tomb was a house for the dead person. Inside it were placed many of the things that the person would have had in life. There were also paintings and sculptures to represent different aspects of their life.

In the graves of poor people, jars and baskets of food and drink were buried with simple tools and equipment. In some of these graves 'soul houses' have been found. These are models of what the person's home may have looked like. In the courtyard of the model house would be placed representations of food and drink to serve the dead in the afterlife.

BURIAL GOODS

Wealthier people and pharaohs would have expensive jewellery, furniture, chests of clothing and other valuable items. They would probably also have buried 'shabtis' with them. These are figures that were specially made for tombs. Shabtis were there to help the dead person in the afterlife, a kind of servant. As the afterlife was supposed to be an idealised replica of life in Egypt, it was believed the deceased person would be called on to work on the land.

Soul houses and shabtis were both made specifically for burial. Models of other everyday objects were also made to be buried with the dead. One of the rituals carried out by the priests was to make these things real for the dead person. Sometimes magic texts or charms were written on the walls of the tomb to help with this.

33

Grave Robbers

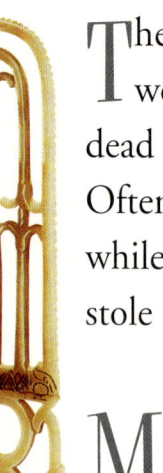

The value of some of the goods that were buried inside the tombs of the dead was too tempting for some people. Often a body was only buried for a short while before grave robbers visited and stole the valuable goods.

Many things were done to try to stop grave robbery. Firstly, inner doors to the burial chambers were locked and the tombs were sealed by placing rocks and rubble inside the entrance passages. Secondly, curses were written on the walls of the tombs to affect anyone who attempted to break in.

Sometimes the person who broke into the tomb was not a simple grave robber, they were not really interested in the valuable items, but in revenge. It was believed that if you could break into the tomb of an enemy, remove his name from the walls and destroy his mummy and any images of him you could make sure that his ka died.

Grave robbery did not only take place during the Ancient Egyptian period. The graves and tombs have been opened, and mummies and objects removed from them for thousands of years. In Europe during the Middle Ages many mummies were ground to a powder and sold as a 'cure all' medicine in the mistaken belief that mummies were coated in a tar-like substance, called 'bitumen', which had miraculous healing properties. The word mummy comes from the Persian word 'mummia' which means bitumen. It was the Persians who originally thought that the black colour of mummies was a result of them being coated with bitumen.

The Valley of the Kings

The tombs of pharaohs were likely targets for grave robbers, and during the period of the New Kingdom tombs were placed in a more secure environment. This is known as the Valley of the Kings. Tuthmosis I, father of Hatshepsut, was the first pharaoh to be buried there.

The Valley of the Kings was a remote and inaccessible valley in Upper Egypt. In this valley the tombs were a series of rooms linked by passages cut into the hillside. The tombs were hundred of metres long, with the farthest room usually containing the mummified body of the pharaoh. The rooms leading to the burial chamber contained the jewellery, furniture, clothing, shabtis and everyday objects the pharaoh would need in his next life.

THE VALLEY OF THE KINGS

Early in November 1922 an Egyptologist discovered what he believed to be the entrance to a tomb in the Valley of the Kings. The man, Howard Carter, had been searching for this tomb for almost 30 years, since he first found a mention of it in an Egyptian text.

Carter believed that the tomb had been virtually undisturbed since it was first sealed, over 3,000 years before. He was almost right. The tomb had been raided very shortly after burial but only the first room had been robbed. Going deeper into the tomb, the men discovered undisturbed treasures and finally, in the burial chamber, the gold coffin of the young pharaoh Tutenkhamun.

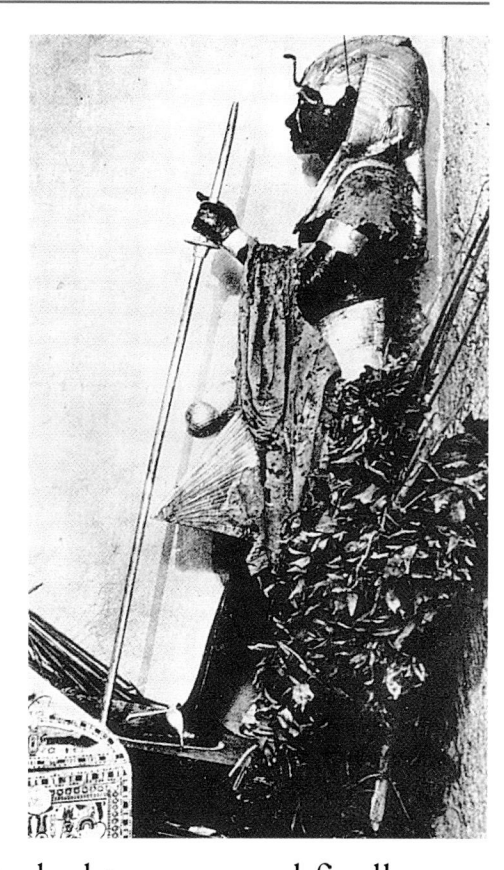

Tutenkhamun

The discovery of the tomb of Tutenkhamun has taught us much about the life and beliefs of the Ancient Egyptians. For the first time, it was possible to make careful records of a tomb. Nothing was removed without first being photographed, catalogued and recorded.

Inside the tomb were more than 2,000 items, including elaborate furniture, ceremonial daggers, chariots, chests and caskets. Many of the items were made from gold. Tutenkhamun's gold coffin weighed over 130 kilograms. One of the most impressive items was the mask covering the face of the mummy. It was also made from gold.

From the mummified body, we can tell that Tutenkhamun was about 18 years old when he died. We think that he was in about the ninth year of his reign as there are jars that contained wine in the tomb with dates from that year. That means he would have been about nine when he became pharaoh.

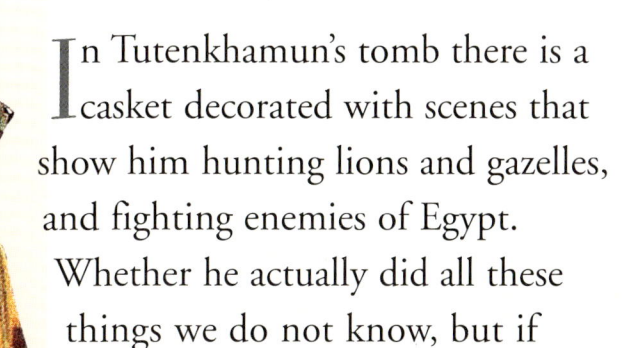

In Tutenkhamun's tomb there is a casket decorated with scenes that show him hunting lions and gazelles, and fighting enemies of Egypt. Whether he actually did all these things we do not know, but if true it suggests that he was an active young man.

His mummy has been X-rayed to try to find out how he died. It was thought at one time that he died from a disease called tuberculosis. However, the X-rays revealed a small piece of broken bone in his head suggesting that he might have been injured in a fall, perhaps from a chariot. Some people have suggested that the bone fragment might have been caused by a blow to the head – that he might have been murdered.

The Rosetta Stone

The Ancient Egyptians devised a system of writing called 'hieroglyphics', that they used for thousands of years. They wrote many documents on 'papyrus', a paper made from reeds. Other hieroglyphs (pictures representing different words or syllables) are found carved into stone or painted on walls.

For many years it was thought that these symbols were a form of writing but no one could understand it. In 1799, a French soldier discovered a stone near Rosetta in Egypt. On the stone was carved the same text in three different versions. One version was in Greek and the two others were different forms of written Ancient Egyptian – one was

THE ROSETTA STONE

hieroglyphics, the other was a sort of short hand form of hieroglyphics called 'Demotic'. Demotic was devised to make the work of scribes quicker and easier.

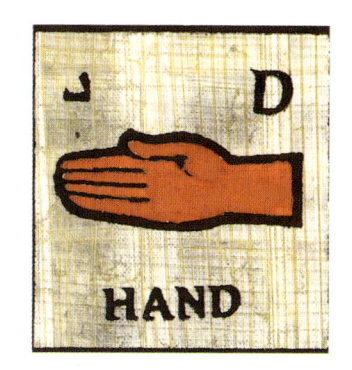

In 1822, a Frenchman named Jean Champollion and the Englishman Thomas Young managed to decipher the secret of the hieroglyphics by studying the Rosetta Stone. They realised that the names of the pharaohs had a loop round them in the text, so by comparing these letters to the Greek letters in the names, they could begin to understand the Egyptian.

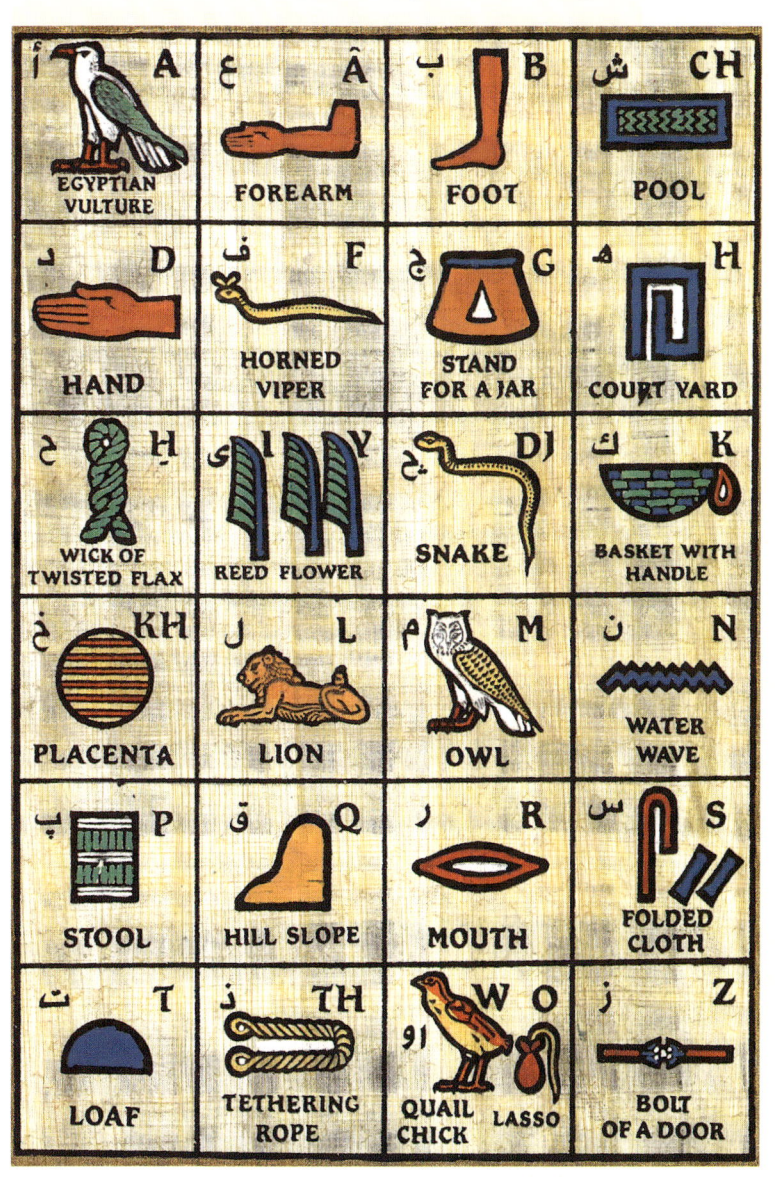

Many hieroglyphs stood for letters or sounds. Sometimes a symbol might stand for a sound like 'sh'. Other hieroglyphs were 'ideograms', that is, they stood for a whole idea or an object.

Cleopatra

Cleopatra VII was the last ruler of a united and independent Egypt, but she was not truly Egyptian. She was Greek.

In 332 BC, Egypt was conquered by Alexander the Great of Greece. He was given the title of Pharaoh, although he did not remain in the country. When Alexander died, Ptolemy Lagus was sent to rule Egypt. Ptolemy gradually became more independent of Greece and took the title of king.

Ptolemy Lagus was succeeded by a number of other Greek rulers of the same name. Under the Ptolemies, Egypt once again became a rich and powerful nation, but there were changes. The government became more like that of Greece and Greek became the official language. New ideas about art and science were introduced from Greece. Although new gods were introduced, the old gods of Ancient Egypt were maintained and worshipped, just as they had been for more than 3,000 years.

CLEOPATRA

Cleopatra VII was the daughter of Ptolemy XII. She was 17 when her father died and she was to rule jointly with her brother Ptolemy XIII, but her brother took over. Cleopatra regained the throne with the help of Julius Caesar and the Romans. Caesar is believed to have been the father of her child Caesarion.

After the death of Julius Caesar, Cleopatra fell in love with another Roman general, called Mark Antony. He came to live with her in Egypt and when the new ruler of Rome declared war on Egypt they fought together. They were defeated and both Mark Antony and Cleopatra committed suicide. Egypt then became ruled directly from Rome, having no king or queen – it was the end of the pharaohs.

Further Information

Places to Visit

Ashmolean Museum - includes displays to illustrate writing, drawing and arts and crafts in Ancient Egypt. Ashmolean Museum, Beaumont Street, Oxford OX1 2PH. Telephone: 01865 278000.

British Museum - includes displays of results from research in bioarcheology: where plant, animal and human materials from the Ancient Egyptian period are studied. These can tell us about the health, disease, medicines, diet and environment of the time. British Museum, Great Russell Street, London, WC1B 3DG. Telephone: 0171 636 1555.

Egypt Centre - about 2,000 objects from Ancient Egypt displayed with explanations in both Welsh and English. Egypt Centre, University College of Swansea, Singleton Park, Swansea, SA2 8PP. Telephone: 01792 295960.

Fitzwilliam Museum - a rich collection of Ancient Egyptian objects. Fitzwilliam Museum, Trumpington Street, Cambridge, CB2 1RB. Telephone: 01223 332993.

Horniman Museum - 100 London Road, Forest Hill, London, SE23 3PQ. Telephone: 0181 699 1872.

Manchester Museum - displays of Ancient Egyptian funerary beliefs and customs and also Ancient Egyptian daily life. Manchester Museum, The University of Manchester, Oxford Road, Manchester, M13 9Pl. Telephone: 0161 275 2630.

Royal Museum of Scotland - displays of mummies, jewellery, ancient food and children's toys. Royal Museum of Scotland, Chambers Street, Edinburgh, EH1 1JF. Telephone: 0131 225 7534.

Swansea Museum - Victoria Road, Maritime Quarter, Swansea, SA1 1SN. Telephone: 01792 653763.

Victoria and Albert Museum - examples of Ancient Egyptian sculpture. Victoria and Albert Museum, Cromwell Road, South Kensington, London, SW7 2RL. Telephone: 0171 938 8500.

FURTHER INFORMATION

Further Reading

Guardians Website - http://www.guardians.net/egypt/egyptreg.htm - extensive information about Ancient Egypt, including features on Tutenkhamun, with a virtual tour of some of the objects found in his tomb.

Ancient Egypt, Dorling Kindersley, 1994

Glorious Treasures: Ancient Egypt by Karen Sullivan, Brockhampton Press, 1997

Rameses II by S.L. Newland, Caxton Editions, 1997

Ancient Egypt by L.A.D. Hawksley, Caxton Editions, 1997

Picture Credits

All pictures courtesy of Foundry Arts, except where indicated:

Page 8 Statue of Ramses II. **Page 10-11** Decorated wooden coffin. **Page 11** Model of a funeral boat. **Page 12-13** Sphinx and Great Pyramid at Cairo. **Page 14** Statue of Horus. **Page 15** Hathor, wall painting in the tomb of Horemheb. **Page 16** Queen Isis. **Page 17** Relief of Osiris. **Page 18** Sandstone relief of a pharaoh. Courtesy of Christie's Images. **Page 19** Statue of Ramses II. **Page 20** Green basalt head of a pharaoh. Courtesy of Christie's Images. **Page 21** Tomb sculpture of armed soldiers marching. Courtesy of The Bridgeman Art Library. **Page 22** Rock sculpture of Ramses II. **Page 23** Ramses II portrayed making an offering. **Page 24** View along the banks of the River Nile. **Page 25** Model of a funeral boat. **Page 26** Ceiling decoration in the tomb of Ramses VI. **Page 27** Painting from the tomb of Nebanoum. Courtesy of Visual Arts Library. **Page 28** Mummies of a cat and a dog (Louvre, Paris). Courtesy of Visual Arts Library. **Page 29** Coffin of Imeneminet (Louvre, Paris). Courtesy of Visual Arts Library. **Page 30** The Great Pyramid, Cairo. **Page 31** Small pyramid, alongside the Great Pyramid, Cairo. **Page 32** Box of Tutankhamen's treasures. **Page 33** Blue-glazed Shabti. Courtesy of Christie's Images. **Page 34** Statue of the servant of the king standing on a panther. **Page 35** Pot for perfumed oil, Tutankhamen's tomb. **Page 36-37** Valley of the Kings. **Page 37** Assorted statues and boxes found in Tutankhamen's tomb. Courtesy of Topham Picturepoint. **Page 38** The eye of Ra. **Page 39** Tutankhamen's gold mask. **Page 40** Example of hieroglyphics on the wall of a temple. **Page 41** The Egyptian alphabet in hieroglyphics. **Page 42** Glazed Egyptian blue wig. Courtesy of Christie's Images. **Page 43** *The meeting of Anthony and Cleopatra.* Courtesy of Christie's Images.

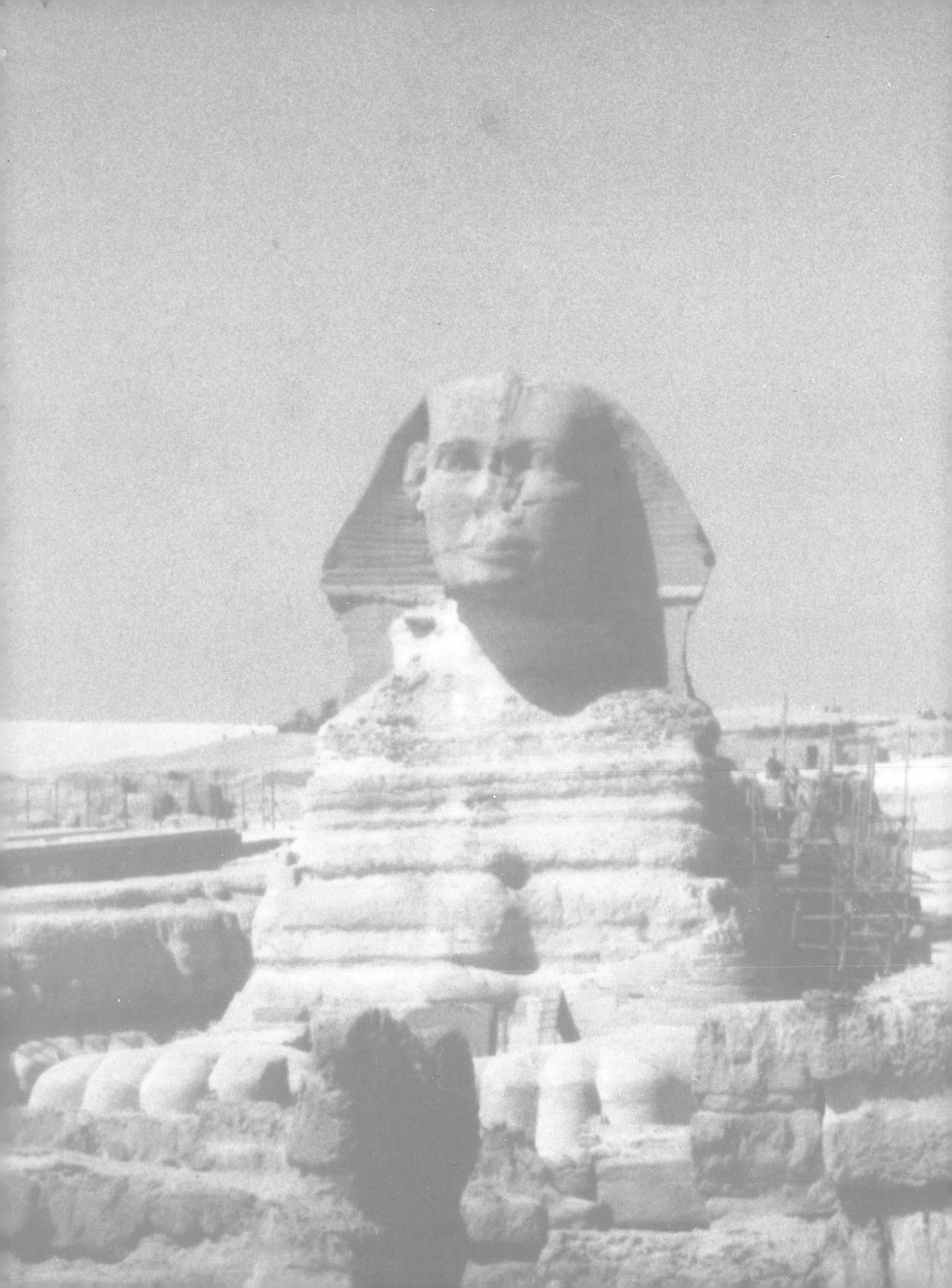